Montana's
MOUNTAIN RANGES

TEXT AND PHOTOS BY RICK AND SUSIE GRAETZ

The Montana Series

NUMBER SIX

PHOTOGRAPHY CONTRIBUTIONS BY:

Randy Beacham ▪ Carr Clifton ▪ Douglass Dye ▪ Chuck Haney ▪ John Lambing ▪ Larry Mayer
Wayne Mumford ▪ Rob Outlaw ▪ John Reddy ▪ Salvatore Vasapolli ▪ George Wuerthner

©2000 Northern Rockies Publishing
Rick and Susie Graetz
P.O. Box 1707, Helena, Montana 59624
norockpub@aol.com

Design by GingerBee Graphics

All color, design and prepress work done in Montana, U.S.A.
Printed in Korea
ISBN 1-891152-09-2

Front Cover:
South face of Granite Peak at 12,799' is where Montana touches the sky.
RICK AND SUSIE GRAETZ

Back Cover:
Snowghosts high in the Whitefish Range
CHUCK HANEY

Bridger Mtns.

near Bozeman.

JOHN LAMBING

TABLE OF CONTENTS

MONTANA'S MOUNTAINS

By Rick and Susie Graetz

They stretch from a 4,058' high point in the Long Pines in the extreme southeast, to 7,705' North-west Peak of the Purcell Mountains in the opposite corner of the state. Sixty-seven separate ranges make up these Montana mountains; and when all the subranges and connecting hills are added, there are actually 131 of them. Thirteen mountain groups rise to 10,000' and higher...more than 586 of the summits exceed 10,000'; sixty surpass 11,000'; and 27 eclipse 12,000' above sea level.

In a contest for the most height, the Beartooth Mountains west of Red Lodge win since they contain all of the 12,000'ers, including Montana's tallest, 12,799' Granite Peak. This lofty mountain range also has 46 peaks reaching 11,000' to 11,999' in height, and 45 climb from 10,000' to 10,999' high. Second place goes to the Madison Range, southwest of Bozeman, which has more than 120 peaks at 10,000' and higher (the Lion's Head summits are included in this total), with 11,316' Hilgard Peak staking claim to the title "Highest Reach Outside of the Beartooth." The Crazy Mountains in south-central Montana, crowned by 11,214' Crazy Peak, come in third and have 25 pinnacles over 10,000'. Contiguous to Beartooth Country, the Absarokas, led by 11,206' Mt. Cowan, form the fourth-highest mountain range. No other Montana mountains come close in terms of having tops over 10,000'...more than 166 Absaroka peaks have that distinction. Between Dillon and Butte, the Pioneers shelter 50 summits over 10,000'. Mt. Tweedy at 11,154' in elevation, makes these lesser known mountains fifth on the list. The Flint Creek Range between Deer Lodge and Philipsburg and its 10,160' Mt. Powell is last on the list of the 13 ranges with peaks over 10,000' above sea level.

Surprisingly, 10,000' crests are absent in some of the awesome chains, such as the Swan, Rocky Mountain Front and Missions. Their highest apexes are only from 8,100' to 9,800', but it is the stunning relief (distance from ground to top) that gives them their stature. Glacier Park mountains (the Lewis and Livingston ranges) have the greatest relief of any range in the state, 10,142' Mt. Stinson and 10,052' Mt. Jackson ascend from 6,800' to 7,000' above their bases.

Blue Mountain, 800' higher than the remote plain between Sidney and Glendive, at a whopping 3,084' in elevation, is the tallest point in northeastern Montana. Then there are the other less obtrusive ranges, such as the Little Sheep and the Big Sheep mountains, a series of hills and eroded badlands between Circle and Glendive, whose highest point at 3,625' is no more than 300' above the adjacent country. West of Ekalaka, the Chalk Buttes are just over 4,000' high and rise only 700' above the prairie floor.

Many Glacier
Valley, Apikuni
Mtn., GNP.
DOUGLASS DYE

The Little Rocky Mountains, south of Malta, can be seen for a long distance. Antone Butte, their highest point at 5,610', is 2,500' higher than surrounding ranchlands. These isolated highlands, as well as others like them—the Bears Paw south of Havre, the Judith and Moccasins next to Lewistown, the Bull Mountains at Roundup, and the Highwoods east of Great Falls—add perspective to the enormous vistas of Montana east of the main Rockies. Compared to the extensive mountains of western Montana, elevations of mountains in the eastern half of the state are low; most of the slopes are less than 5,500' (the only exception being the 8,600' rise of the Big Snowy Mountains south of Lewistown).

Each place has its own characteristics and offers new areas to explore. Old mining camps and ghost towns are found in the Garnet, Castle, Elkhorn, Flint Creek, Judith and other ranges. The Pryors are known for their wild horses and desert environment, the Cabinets for the giant cedars, and the Big Snowies for their ice caves and the best long-distance views in the state. Glaciers are found in the Absarokas, Beartooths, Crazies, Swans, Missions and, of course, Glacier National Park. Millions of fossils can be discovered in the Trilobite Range of the Bob Marshall. Snow ghosts appear in the Whitefish and Swan ranges, and the largest native herd of mountain goats in the U.S. walks the ledges of the Rocky Mountain Front.

There are several lifetimes worth of Montana's mountains to climb and explore. One man, Cedron Jones of Helena, had (as of the summer of 2000) summitted 180 of Montana's 200 tallest mountains. Overall, he has been atop 900 of the state's pinnacles. He also claims the distinction of having climbed almost all of the uppermost points in each of Montana's 131 mountain ranges (main and subranges).

Toughest climb for the Helena man: 12,799' Granite Peak. Most technical range: Glacier Park peaks, as well as some in the Bitterroots.

CEDRON JONES'S 100 HIGHEST MONTANA SUMMITS CRITERIA FOR MEASUREMENT

Jones started making his way to Montana's wide roof in 1973 when he scaled 6,167' Squaw Peak near his home in Heron in northwest Montana. A serious interest to bag the 100 loftiest places started in 1985 when he went to work putting protective edges on each of the 3,010 USGS topographic maps that cover Montana. He realized by using these quadrangles, he could assemble a data base to ascertain the "top 100;" his reasoning... "how could you climb them all without identifying them?"

A system was needed. What do you call a peak? Some maps don't have a point elevation, but the contours tell how high something is. Cedron identified three options...consider only named points, all those places with elevations assigned by the US Geological Survey, or a minimum rise from below a higher neighbor. The self proclaimed "peak bagger" chose the third guideline and established his criteria...the point had to be at least 400' above a ridgeline if it was connected, via that spine, to a higher peak. Others have "lower standards;" the Colorado Mountain Club uses 300' in determining the 14,000'ers and the Appalachian Club uses 200' in cataloging their 4,000' points.

Page 9 displays "Cedron's 100."

Big Belt Mtns.
near Beaver Creek.
JOHN REDDY

In the
Anaconda-
Pintler
Wilderness.
RICK AND SUSIE GRAETZ

MONTANA'S 100 HIGHEST MOUNTAINS ACCORDING TO CEDRON JONES

1. Granite Pk	12,799	Beartooth		51. Mt Cowen	11,212	Absaroka
2. Mt Wood	12,649	Beartooth		52. Echo Pk	11,211	Madison
3. Castle Mtn	12,612	Beartooth		53. Crazy Pk	11,209	Crazy Mtns
4. Whitetail Pk	12,551	Beartooth		54. Imp Pk	11,200 +	Madison
5. Silver Run Pk	12,542	Beartooth		55. Two Sisters	11,190	Beartooth
6. Castle Rock Spire	12,540	Beartooth		56. Lone Mtn	11,162	Madison
7. Tempest Mtn	12,469	Beartooth		57. Tweedy Mtn	11,154	Pioneer
8. Mt Peal	12,409	Beartooth		58. Torrey Mtn	11,147	Pioneer
9. Castle Rock Mtn	12,401	Beartooth		59. Chalice Pk	11,146	Beartooth
10. Bowback Mtn	12,351	Beartooth		60. Eighteenmile Pk	11,125	Beaverhead
11. Beartooth Mtn	12,351	Beartooth		61. Pk W of Mt Hague	11,103	Beartooth
12. Mt Villard	12,345	Beartooth		62. Hodges Mtn	11,087	Beartooth
13. Mt Hague	12,323	Beartooth		63. Pk N of Summit Mtn	11,086	Beartooth
14. Glacier Pk	12,320 +	Beartooth		64. Grass Mtn	11,052	Beartooth
15. Spirit Mtn	12,283	Beartooth		65. Pk W of Koch Pk	11,049	Madison
16. Sundance Mtn	12,262	Beartooth		66. Cottonwood	11,024	Beaverhead
17. Mt Rearguard	12,204	Beartooth		67. Pk NW of Imp Pk	11,000 +	Madison
18. Cairn Mtn	12,200 +	Beartooth		68. Gallatin Pk	11,000 +	Madison
19. Snowbank Mtn	12,084	Beartooth		69. Monument Pk	10,995	Absaroka
20. Mystic Mtn	12,080 +	Beartooth		70. Pk NW of Summit	10,972	Beartooth
21. Sky Pilot Mtn	12,047	Beartooth		71. Electric Pk	10,969	Gallatin
22. "Metcalf Mtn"	11,977	Beartooth		72. Garfield Mtn	10,961	Beaverhead
23. Sylvan Pk	11,935	Beartooth		73. Snowy Pk	10,960 +	Beartooth
24. Mt Inabnit	11,928	Beartooth		74. Pk E of Rough Lake	10,952	Beartooth
25. Pk NW of Snowbank	11,848	Beartooth		75. Black Mtn	10,941	Absaroka
26. Mt Wilse	11,831	Beartooth		76. Pk W of Expdtn. Pass	10,938	Madison
27. Stillwater Plateau	11,817	Beartooth		77. Iddings Pk	10,936	Crazy Mtns
28. Wolf Mtn	11,800 +	Beartooth		78. Pk W of Sentinel Pk	10,930	Madison
29. Twin Pks	11,793	Beartooth		79. Emigrant Pk	10,921	Absaroka
30. Summit Mtn	11,704	Beartooth		80. Pk NW of Mt Wilse	10,920 +	Beartooth
31. Pk N of Sawtooth	11,680 +	Beartooth		81. The Needles	10,880 +	Absaroka
32. Pk S of Arch Lake	11,576	Beartooth		82. Sphinx Mtn	10,876	Madison
33. Iceberg Pk	11,552	Beartooth		83. Saddleback Mtn	10,876	Beartooth
34. Pk S of Little Park	11,505	Beartooth		84. Tunnel Ridge	10,852	Madison
35. Sawtooth Mtn	11,488	Beartooth		85. Pk SE of Smeller Lk	10,840 +	Crazy Mtns
36. Little Park Mtn	11,480 +	Beartooth		86. Pk SE of Sheepherder Pk	10,840 +	Absaroka
37. Mt Hole-in-the-Wall	11,478	Beartooth		87. Pk S of Expedition Pass	10,835	Madison
38. Pk 2S of Little Park	11,443	Beartooth		88. Pk N of Koch Pk	10,829	Madison
39. Thunder Mtn	11,441	Beartooth		89. Pk E of Italian Pk	10,821	Beaverhead
40. Pk E of Summit Mtn	11,440 +	Beartooth		90. Pk NE of Imp Pk	10,809	Madison
41. Lonesome Mtn	11,400 +	Beartooth		91. Pk N of Avalanche Lk	10,800 +	Madison
42. Pk SE of Big Mtn	11,380	Beartooth		92. West Goat Pk	10,793	Anaconda
43. Pk S of Mt Villard	11,379	Beartooth		93. West Boulder Plateau	10,778	Absaroka
44. Big Mtn	11,371	Beartooth		94. Baldy Mtn	10,773	Beaverhead
45. Hilgard Pk	11,316	Madison		95. Cedar Mtn	10,768	Madison
46. Tumble Mtn	11,314	Beartooth		96. Pk E of Koch Pk	10,764	Madison
47. Koch Pk	11,293	Madison		97. Pk NE of Mt Cowen	10,762	Absaroka
48. Mt Douglas	11,282	Beartooth		98. Lake Mtn	10,762	Beartooth
49. Mt Fox	11,245	Beartooth		99. Pk S of Woodward	10,760 +	Madison
50. Pk E of Little Park	11,245	Beartooth		100. Conical Pk	10,748	Crazy Mtns

Beargrass and
the Chinese Wall.
CARR CLIFTON

Mission Mtns.
from the
National Bison
Range.
CHUCK HANEY

MOUNTAINS OF THE BOB MARSHALL COUNTRY

THE BOB MARSHALL, SCAPEGOAT AND GREAT BEAR WILDERNESS AREAS

West of Augusta, Choteau, Bynum and Dupuyer, the Montana prairie is abruptly terminated by the spectacular towering walls of the Rocky Mountain Front. For 110 miles, stretching from Glacier National Park south to Rogers Pass, these craggy limestone barriers serve as the eastern rampart of the Bob Marshall Country.

The magnificence of "The Front" is crowned by its highest summit, 9,392' Rocky Mountain Peak. The sights of sharp reefs, clear streams and lofty peaks on the Rocky Mountain Front offer a proper prelude to what lies ahead through the few tight, deep canyons that serve as gateways to the wildlands beyond.

From Ear Mountain, a prominent Front Range peak, an eagle flies 60 miles before reaching the slopes of the equally impressive Swan Range, "The Bob's" western flank.

Valleys of the Two Medicine, Sun and Dearborn rivers separate the Rocky Mountain Front from the Continental Divide Range. The reefs, peaks and ridges of the Divide include Scapegoat Mountain and the Chinese Wall, places that represent the essence of wilderness to many people.

The Chinese Wall is a most unusual and magnificent formation. This 13-mile-long escarpment rises immediately 1,000' above its east side, then slopes for several miles westward down to the White River. Its high point is 8,576' Cliff Mt.

Scapegoat Mountain, a three-mile-long reef with precipitous walls ascending above Half Moon Park, tops out at 9,204'.

Heading westward, note that the Middle Fork of the Flathead River and the Spotted Bear River separate the Continental Divide Range from the Flathead Range. The Flathead Mountains extend north from the Chinese Wall for 60 miles through The Bob, to Glacier. Their western border is the valley of the South Fork of the Flathead and Hungry Horse Reservoir. Great Northern Mountain, 8,705', is its highest reach.

Some of this wilderness's most remote country lies south of Spotted Bear River. Silvertip Mountain, 8,890' and honeycombed with caves, and a cluster of 8,000' peaks, follows down to the Flathead Alps, just above White River Pass and the Chinese Wall. The South Fork of the Flathead is to the west of this wild area.

The wide valleys of the South Fork of the Flathead, and the Danaher River and meadows, set apart the central group from the westernmost mountains of the Bob Marshall, the Swan Range. The Swan slopes steeply up on its west face, from the Swan Valley. They form a wall rising through dense forests to rocky, snow capped tops. Holland Peak, 9,356' (west of Condon) is their highest summit. The Jewel Basin Hiking Area is in the northern segment of the Swan.

The Swan Range turns eastward as it reaches the Blackfoot Valley on the south. Here a mass of mountains stretches east past the small town of Lincoln to Rogers Pass and the Continental Divide, and forms The Bob's southern perimeter. Red Mountain, 9,411', the loftiest peak in the entire wilderness mountain complex, is in the heart of this group of summits.

THE MISSION MOUNTAINS

It hits you at once, this very dramatic view of the Mission Mountains…all 7,000' of vertical rise from St. Ignatius to the top of 9,880' McDonald Peak, the highest summit in the range. This abrupt skyward reach suddenly appears to drivers as Highway 93 crests a steep hill northeast of the town of Ravalli.

On the north, at Bigfork, these Missions begin their gradual ascent as forested hills, looking much the same as many of the other lower mountains of the western part of the state, but as they progress south the elevation increases dramatically. Here, summits soar far above timberline, culminating in spectacular jagged peaks, some cradling glaciers on their north side. Along the west slope, the overall relief is the greatest found anywhere in the state, upwards of 6,000'–7,000' from the southern Mission Valley floor.

The topography of the Missions is a compact version of Glacier National Park. The high country landscape is a mix of nearly 200 aqua-blue lakes, cascading waterfalls, glacier-fed streams, steep snowfields, ice-carved ridges and peaks, and colorful sedimentary rocks.

The southern half of this spectacular mountain chain enjoys designated wilderness status…the Mission Mountain Wilderness Area and the contiguous Mission Mountain Tribal Wilderness.

RATTLESNAKE MOUNTAINS

The Rattlesnakes are Missoula's mountains, dominating the northeast horizon of this university town. The land is protected by the Rattlesnake Wilderness Area, as well as the Rattlesnake National Recreational Area and the Tribal Primitive Area to the north. Trails meander throughout it. McCloud Peak at 8,620' is the highest summit. Stuart Peak, a favorite trek, is 7,960' high. More than 50 creeks and 30 lakes grace the upper reaches of the Wilderness section. The northern segment of the area, managed by the Confederated Salish-Kootenai Tribes, is off limits to all but tribal members because it is a sacred site.

Missoula Snowbowl Ski Area sits in the Rattlesnake Mountains.

NINEMILE DIVIDE

A range of peaks that separate a segment of the Clark Fork River drainage from the Ninemile Creek drainage just to the north of Missoula.

Twin Lakes from
Stuart Pk. in the
Rattlesnake
Wilderness.
GEORGE WUERTHNER

Grinnell Lake
in Grinnell Valley,
GNP.
DOUGLASS DYE

THE MOUNTAINS OF GLACIER NATIONAL PARK

Of all of Montana's mountain ranges, the peaks of Glacier National Park are undeniably the most beautiful. The area serves as a living textbook of the forces of glaciation and erosion. Glaciers of ice ages past did their finest work here.

Essentially these awesome mountains are an enormous slab of sedimentary rock that came here from elsewhere during geologic history. Like the Bob Marshall Wilderness Area ranges to the south, this northern extension of the Lewis Overthrust (a geographic term meaning older rocks sliding up and over younger ones in this particular area) was pushed eastward by incredible forces within the earth, leaving behind the trenches that became the Flathead and North Fork valleys. Estimates are that they were moved about 35 to 50 miles from their original location.

An estimated 37 active alpine glaciers, which cling to high cirques and north facing headwalls, are scattered throughout this 1,538-square-mile preserve. The largest is the 430-acre Blackfoot Glacier. Grinnell, 217 acres, and Sperry, 220 acres, are visited by hundreds of trekkers every year. These and the other ice fields throughout the peaks, are not remnants of past ice ages, but rather formed in more recent years. At the current rate of warming and melting, it is estimated that all of them could be gone by 2030. At one time, glaciers filled most of the area's valleys to the depths of 3,000' and spread out far beyond the mountains.

The force and cutting power of the ice left behind over 200 lakes, countless waterfalls, towering rock walls 3,000' to 4,000' high, and magnificent U-shaped valleys. These results gave the park its name.

Glacier is divided into two ranges...the eastern 65-mile-long Lewis Range and the 35-mile-long Livingston Range to the west. The loftiest summit in the park, 10,466' Mount Cleveland, is in the Lewis group. Kintla Peak, 10,101', is the tallest of the Livingston apexes.

Although not as high as southern Montana's mountains, these massifs seem taller because of their relief. Cleveland's north face, rising 6,700' in four miles, has the distinction of being Montana's steepest vertical ascent.

The only road to cross the park is the narrow and winding, but stunning, Going-To-The-Sun Road. Completed in 1932 after 11 years of construction, this scenic byway, and engineering marvel, gives access to some of the same type of mountain scenery that backcountry wanderers experience. It is usually open from mid-June until late September. Deep snows and drifts, which by spring pile to depths of 80' and more, block the route the rest of the year.

Nearly all of Glacier is wilderness backcountry, and 700 miles of hiking trails lead to some of the grandest sights in North America.

Nearly two-thirds of the park's mountains are covered with thick evergreen forests. On the west side, in the area of Lake McDonald, plentiful moisture allows for the tall Western red cedars to thrive. Heavy forests on the slopes of the big peaks in the northern part of the park are remote and provide excellent grizzly bear habitat. Most other big-game animals call this entire terrain home...black bear, deer, elk, bighorn sheep, mountain goats, cougars, and all the small critters, make a good living here.

The Yaak Valley
from Hensley
Face.
RANDY BEACHAM

THE WHITEFISH RANGE

A major range, stretching 60 miles north of Columbia Falls to the Canadian line, most of its peaks are in the 7,000' area, but the relief of up to 4,000' on the west side is impressive. The highest summit in the Montana segment (part of the Whitefish Range extends into Canada) is Nasukoin Mountain at 8,095'.

Major portions of the range remain roadless. Ten Lakes Scenic Area was established for hiking, but the Northfork Wildlands—consisting of Tuchuck, Mount Hefty and Thompson Seton—lack lasting federal wilderness protection. Their heavy timber provides excellent grizzly bear habitat.

The range is bordered by the North Fork of the Flathead River and the peaks of Glacier Park to the east, and the Tobacco Valley on their western edge.

The most famous attraction in the Whitefish Range is the Big Mountain Ski Area, a major destination resort.

THE CABINET MOUNTAINS

The Cabinet Mountains, just to the west of Libby, are the dominant range of northwestern Montana. They extend about 80 miles along a northwest-southeast axis and are bordered by the Idaho state line on the west, the Clark Fork River and Hwy 200 on the south, Thompson River on the east, and the Kootenai River and Highway 2 on the north.

The Cabinet Mountain Wilderness forms the core of the range. This 35-mile-long wild area of nearly 100,000 acres consists of jagged peaks, high lake basins and open country, with spectacular alpine views. The summits are relatively low, but surrounding elevations are among the lowest in Montana, and so the resulting relief creates formidable-looking mountains. The highest point in the range is 8,712' Snow Shoe Peak. The Cabinets themselves are the highest mountains between Glacier National Park and the Cascade Range of Washington to the west. As such, they form one of the first major mountain barriers to eastward-flowing Pacific storms that therefore drop up to 100" of precipitation here each year.

The mountains of the southeast portion of the Cabinets are less rugged than the wilderness summits. Several peaks are more than 7,000' high, including 7,429' Mount Headley.

The Bull River Valley separates the Cabinet Mountain Wilderness Area from the rest of the range to the northwest. The tops of this segment are the lowest in the range, reaching elevations of about 6,500'.

Many of the peaks and the surrounding forest lands of the northwest part of the state have been heavily logged; the country surrounding the Cabinets is no exception. Nonetheless though, 75,000 acres of this area—the Scotchman Peaks in the West Cabinets—are pristine wildlands. Ross Creek and its giant cedar trees (some are more than 8' in diameter and 175' tall) are in this area. Savage Mountain, 6,900', is the highest pinnacle in the West Cabinet/Scotchman Peaks. From here the range slopes downward and north to 1,802' above sea level, the lowest point in the state—where the Kootenai River leaves Montana just west of Troy.

PURCELL MOUNTAINS

Home of the Yaak River Valley and the Northwest Peak Scenic Area, the Purcells rise in the extreme northwest corner of Montana. They're just north of Libby and the Kootenai River, Idaho is to their west, Canada to the north, and 35-mile-long Lake Kookanuska stretches along the eastern perimeter.

As elsewhere in northwestern Montana, elevations here are relatively low. The highest mountains of the Purcells are found in and around the Northwest Peak Scenic Area. Northwest Peak, 7,705', is their highest pinnacle.

Much of the area is roaded and logged, but the Northwest Peak Scenic Area has been set aside as an area protected from timbering, and contains several lake basins (including seven high lakes), and superb mountain scenery. The remains of a 1930s lookout tower offer big vistas of the surrounding Yaak River Wildlands as well as far north and into Canada.

Across a labyrinth of roads and clear-cut forests, the prominent points of Purcell Peak and 7,243' Mount Henry stand out.

Just beyond the Northwest Peaks Area, and a few miles to the west and above the Yaak River, the 25-mile-long roadless Buckhorn Ridge—ascending between 6,000' and 6,5000'—is an important wildlife sanctuary.

SALISH MOUNTAINS

This range of timbered hills and mountains runs for 100 miles from just south of Eureka to the west of Polson, and Flathead Lake. The highest summits are short of 7,000'. Named for the Salish Indians, these mountains feature many large lakes—including Lake Mary Ronan, Little Bitterroot, McGregor, Hubbert, Thompson, Ashley and Talley—all well-known recreation areas. Blacktail Mountain, 6,757', just west of Lakeside, is the state's newest ski area. Baldy Mountain, 7,464', and just west of Hot Springs in the extreme southern end of the range, is the highest peak.

Bull River
Valley and the
Cabinet Mtns.
RICK AND SUSIE GRAETZ

Beartooth high
country near
Martin Lake Basin.
RICK AND SUSIE GRAETZ

Viewing peaks
south of Elephant
Mtn., Absaroka-
Beartooth.
GEORGE WUERTHNER

ABSAROKA-BEARTOOTH MOUNTAINS—THE TOP OF MONTANA

It's an awesome and wild landscape...the roof of Montana where the highest summits in the state soar above an already–cloud-piercing plateau.

This land in the sky was named in part for the Absaroka people...the Crow Indians. The Beartooth Spire (called "Na pietsay" by the Crow), and seen from the Beartooth Highway, was responsible for the over-all Beartooth name.

The AB, as it is sometimes called, consists of two distinct ranges separated by the Boulder River as it flows north out of the mountains through a precipitous gorge to the Yellowstone River.

The Beartooth crags climb to the east and consist of much of the land above treeline. Glaciers fill high cirques and cling to north-facing headwalls of some of the highest ridges and summits. More than 400" of annual snow help maintain perennial snowfields and glaciers, and are the reason why much of the high country is still under significant snow cover into late July.

Somewhat lower, but very rugged, and with a heavier forest cover, the Absarokas rise on the west side of the Boulder. They see fewer visitors than the Beartooth, and are a bit tougher to navigate.

More than three-fourths of the AB is above timberline and elevated enough to have tundra soil. Nine major drainages pour out of the higher reaches, giving the Yellowstone River, between Yellowstone National Park and Billings, one-third of its flow. Estimates of the number of lakes is near 1,000. Overall, the unroaded segments of the complex cover more than 1,135,000 acres. Most of it, 920,324 acres, is in designated wilderness.

Together, the Absaroka-Beartooth boasts of more than 120 peaks over 10,000' in elevation. Twenty-nine of them top 12,000', including Montana's highest, 12,799' Granite Peak.

Owing to its elevation, this lofty terrain is scoured by wind, and at times has ferocious weather. Summer thunder-and-lightning storms, accompanied by hail, can be frightening at times, and snow is possible even in July and August.

Once up in the rolling alpine landscape, though, a hiker reaches a pristine place. Here is a most magnificent environment of lakes, rushing streams, waterfalls, snow and ice and, in the warm months, a wildflower display that's among the best in the Northern Rockies. Great views spanning idyllic mountain panoramas are everywhere. It is a world unto itself!

Numerous trails provide access along the entire fringe of the Absaroka-Beartooth. Up in the high terrain, they disappear. These cloud-swept areas, relatively easy to negotiate, require a map and compass. And elevation gains, as much as distance, need to be considered when planning a trip.

North face of
Granite Pk.
RICK AND SUSIE GRAETZ

GRANITE PEAK—MONTANA'S HIGHEST

It is all a mountain should be…remote and majestic. Sheer walls on all sides and crevassed glaciers flowing from its upper reaches present an awesome sight. At 12,799', Montana's Granite Peak stands out as the patriarch of "the roof of Montana," the Beartooth Range of the south-central part of the state.

The one-million-acre Absaroka Beartooth Wilderness boasts 28 peaks above 12,000' in elevation. Granite is one of seven of these found in a closely-grouped chain that includes Hidden Glacier—12,377', Glacier Peak—12,351', Mount Villard—12,319', Tempest Mountain—12,478', Mystic Mountain—12,063' and Mount Peal—12,002'.

The heights of Granite and the surrounding summits piqued the interest of early-day Beartooth explorers and mountaineers. In late July 1898, a pioneering expedition to these big peaks was led by geologist and mining engineer James Kimball. He was searching for minerals and planned to map the region between Cooke City and Nye. Bad weather disrupted the mapping, and no precious metals were found. The group did make an attempt on Granite Peak, but were stopped at the 11,447' level (estimated by their aneroid barometer).

Perhaps the person with the most interest in exploring the Beartooth and climbing Montana's loftiest peak was Fred Inabnit (Mount Inabnit, south of East Rosebud Lake was named in his honor). His first sojourn in these mountains was in 1907; then, in 1910, he approached Granite with the thought of scaling it. He scanned the east ridge and concluded that there had to be a better route. After crossing Granite Creek and the pass to Sky Top Drainage on the peak's east and south sides, his party was turned back by an intense August snowstorm.

Again, in 1922, Inabnit led five well-equipped climbers to Granite, approaching from the south by way of Sky Top Creek. They came within 300' of the top before being halted by sheer walls.

The undaunted Inabnit returned once more, in 1923, after persuading the Forest Service to participate in a joint climbing venture. From a camp on Avalanche lake, in upper Granite Creek (southeast side), the expedition split into two assault teams. They spent the first day making a reconnaissance of the mountain, and concluded that there was no easy way to the top. The next morning, Inabnit led his group into the Sky Top for another try at the south face. Forest Service legend Elers Koch took the other climbers up the east ridge. Inabnit and his team were again blocked by steep walls when they heard the triumphant shouts of the rangers above, and that was how Granite Peak was first climbed that August 23, 1923.

Ascending Granite today is just as exciting, and almost as challenging as it was at the turn of the century. Altitude, weather, and very rugged and precipitous terrain, place our state's highest summit and its environs among the most adventuresome areas to climb in Montana.

The peak can be approached from several points. The south side is best reached by going from Cooke City to the Sky Top Lakes. The most popular route, and the one that leads to the so called "easiest climb" (on the east face and also to the north face) is from Fishtail to Mystic Lake and the Froze-to-Death Plateau. A trail up Phantom Creek from East Rosebud Lake is also used to get to these same places. All these routes are shown on Rocky Mountain Surveys' Alpine/Cooke City map.

And you can get the more detailed 7.5 minute U.S.GS quads at your local outdoor shop as well. Falcon Press's *Hiking Montana* has a good description of the Mystic Lake access.

There are four major routes to climb the peak: the east face route, the north face, a couple of spines on the southeast side, and the south face. The south and north faces are the most difficult. No passage on Granite offers a hands-in-the-pocket walk. All approaches and pitches are steep, requiring a great deal of physical effort. Granite Peak should never be considered as a first mountain for novice climbers unless they are accompanied by at least one experienced mountaineer. A knowledge of route finding, belaying and rappelling techniques, and the use of an ice ax, are necessary. An experienced group can do the east face without equipment—other than an ice ax needed for the snowbridge encountered part of the way up. A 150' length of at least a 9-mm rope, for safety purposes, would be good to have.

Granite presents many hazards, including intense rain or snow storms that can strike at a moments notice, high winds, slick boulders, falling rocks, and the dangers of hypothermia. Dressing properly with layers, using quality camping gear, and having some idea of the long-range weather conditions will help provide you with a great experience in spite of the inherent dangers on, and around, this very formidable mountain.

PRYOR MOUNTAINS

A red desert, ice caves, and wild horses are symbols of this most unique piece of Montana's mountain country. The island-like Pryor Mountains of the south-central part of the state are made up of two high ridges, each about 20 miles across. The northern stretch is within the boundaries of the Crow Reservation. Here, the highest points—a little over 7,300'—descend gradually to lower, timbered buttes.

Ice caves, and the 31,000-acre Pryor Mountain National Wild Horse Range, highlight the southern part, where the summits top out over 8,700'. A dramatic plunge of 5,000' to a desert environment exists at the southern most tip. These areas are open to the public.

An 8,500'-high reef of limestone with sharp drop-offs makes up most of the west side of the range. The east face declines from wooded ridges and cliffs to lower hills that are abruptly ended by the sharp walls of Bighorn Canyon National Recreation Area.

This raised landscape is unlike any other place in the state. Its diversity is unequaled, ranging from high desert to subalpine terrain in a short distance.

BIGHORN MOUNTAINS

The most sacred of mountains in Crow Country, this 120-mile range has only its northernmost 20 miles in Montana.

East face of
the Pryor Mtns.
above Bighorn
Canyon.
RICK AND SUSIE GRAETZ

To live at the foot of the mountains

is to view beauty every day.

Bozeman and
the MSU campus
beneath the
Bridger Mtns.
ROB OUTLAW

Up to 50 miles across, the Bighorns start a gradual climb to 9,000' from the valley of the Little Bighorn River as a series of fissured wide ridges. The upper reaches of the Montana segment of the Bighorns are relatively flat. Relief from the bottoms of the two major canyons that split the area—Black Canyon to the east and Big Bull Elk Canyon on the west—ranges from 2,000'–2,500'. These deep ravines drain to the Bighorn Canyon as they slice through the sheer northern edge of the range.

CRAZY MOUNTAINS

Nowhere else in Montana is the transition from prairie to mountains so dramatic. In a 20-mile span from the river bottoms of the Yellowstone to the pinnacle of 11,214' Crazy Peak, the terrain rises more than 7,000'. The Crazies are only about 30 miles deep and 15 miles across, but are the sentinel on the distant horizon seen from all points east.

They are the third-highest range in the state. The valleys of the Yellowstone and Shield rivers set them apart from the Absarokees to the south and the Bridgers in the west.

THE BRIDGER RANGE

North of Bozeman, and west across the Shields Valley from the Crazies, the 25-mile-long Bridger Range rises to its highest summit, 9,665' Sacajawea Peak. The Bridgers are best known for having one of the best powder skiing areas in Montana, Bridger Bowl.

Much of this chain is a long steep ridgeline, but in its north, near Sacajawea, some good hiking is possible.

BANGTAIL MOUNTAINS

Locally named, this short, low range of mountains just to the east of the Bridger Range is popular for bike riding and hiking.

REESE AND OIL HILLS

A grouping of 6,000' hills to the west of the Crazy Mountains, and near Ringling.

Como Pks.
in the Bitterroot
Range.
RICK AND SUSIE GRAETZ

In the Bitterroot
Range, the
Beaverhead Mtns.
near Lemhi Pass.
JOHN LAMBING

BITTERROOT RANGE

INCLUDES THE BITTERROOT MOUNTAINS, BEAVERHEAD MOUNTAINS, ITALIAN PEAKS AND CENTENNIAL MOUNTAINS

At a point in northwest Montana where the Cabinet Gorge allows the Clark Fork River to continue its journey beyond the state, forested slopes rise abruptly, 2,300' above the water, to create the northern tip of the Bitterroot Range. Twisting and turning, ascending and lowering, the crest stretches south for 470 miles to form almost the entire Montana-Idaho border. Halfway along, at Lost Trail Pass (named early–20th century surveyors who lost their way near here), the Continental Divide joins and stays with this high barrier the rest of the way.

Three subgroups compose the main range. From their beginnings, in the north, to Lost Trail Pass, these are named the Bitterroot Mountains. South to Monida Pass, they are the Beaverheads. At Monida they become the Centennials and turn east to the vicinity of Henry's Lake, Raynolds Pass, and the terminus of the Bitterroot Range.

Montana's largest mountain chain drains a wide area, discharging water to both the Pacific Ocean and the Gulf of Mexico. On the north side of Lost Trail Pass, the Bitterroots and Sapphires form a bowl spawning the Bitterroot River and the start of a 245-mile-long north-by-northwest conduit for runoff from the east face of the range, which meets the Pacific via the Clark Fork of the Columbia.

Lost Trail Pass serves as the separating point for the watershed of the Bitterroots. All flow from its south connects with major tributaries of the Missouri, such as the Big Hole, Beaverhead and Red Rock rivers, and eventually pours into the Gulf of Mexico.

From the Cabinet Gorge southward to Lolo Pass (west of Missoula), the 6,000'–7,000' peaks are relatively low and heavily tree-covered. This is timber country and, as a result, quite a few logging roads get close to the divide. Lookout Pass, a major thoroughfare across the mountains, connects Montana with Idaho and Washington. Pockets of wildlands, including the proposed Great Burn wilderness, spot the area.

At Lolo Pass, some of Montana's most rugged summits—ranging from 9,000' to 10,000', including 10,157' Trapper Peak—begin their climb to the sky. Towering jagged pinnacles, precipitous walls, and a series of long U-shaped glacier-carved canyons make up the Montana side of the landscape. This is the section most people associate with the Bitterroots. Extending to Lost Trail Pass, much of the range is included in the 1.25-million-acre Selway-Bitterroot Wilderness.

South of the joining of the Continental and Bitterroot divides, the peaks of the Beaverhead section are less rugged than those to the north, but they are higher and more massive. Many are over 10,000', including 10,620' Homer Youngs rising above the Big Hole Valley. The mountains to the valley's west are part of the proposed West Big Hole Wilderness Area. For the most part they are unroaded, and footpaths lead to more than 30 high-country lakes.

Somewhat lower peaks south of the Big Hole watershed allow for a few roads to touch the Beaverhead crest. Lemhi Pass, the route Meriwether Lewis of the Lewis and Clark Expedition used to cross the Continental Divide for the first time, is here. After Lemhi Pass, the tops sweep upward again reaching 11,141' at Eighteen Mile Peak. Italian Peak, the southernmost point in Montana, tops out at 10,998'. These mountains look down on some of the state's least populated space, the Big Sheep and Nicholia Basin. In the mid-1800s, pioneers and gold seekers crossed from the west and south into this sagebrush terrain on their way to gold fields farther the north. One of these, Bannack Pass, was the crossing for the Bannack Freight Road that was established in 1862, and its route still exists today.

On the east edge of the basin and just beyond Four Eyes Canyon, the Lima Peaks—and Garfield Mountain Roadless Area—Red Conglomerate Peak complex completes the Beaverheads. Most of these summits exceed 10,000' and then scale down, eastward, to 6,870' Monida Pass.

Barren windswept foothills east of Monida lead the way back up again to the heights. The Centennial Mountains—reaching to 9,000' and higher—carry the final 40-mile stretch of the Montana-Idaho border and the Montana segment of the Continental Divide. Below their north face, the Centennial Valley and Red Rocks Lake National Wildlife Refuge, home to the trumpeter swan, spread out. Red Rock Pass, the eastern gateway to the Red Rocks, terminates the rise of the Bitterroot Mountains.

COEUR D' ALENE MOUNTAINS

A part of the Bitterroot Range, this subrange extends for almost 75 miles, with peaks ranging from 5,000' to 7,000', between the lower Clark Fork River and the St. Regis River south of Thompson Falls.

PIONEER MOUNTAINS

One of only six ranges in the state with summits over 11,000', the Pioneers are separated into east and west by the Wise River, and bordered on three sides by the U-shaped channel of the Big Hole River. Dillon is off to the southeast, and Wisdom and the Big Hole Valley guard the range to the west. The East Pioneers are the highest and most glaciated of the two sets of ranges. Tweedy Peak, at 11,154', and Torrey at 11,147', are the two highest summits. Many trails crisscross this seldom-visited group of mountains. The West Pioneers are more rounded than their eastern counterparts, but are no less wild.

More than 80 lakes dot these mountains' upper reaches. And an approximately 500-year-old stand of lodgepole pine, one of the oldest known, survives here.

RUBY MOUNTAINS

A 15-mile-long range southwest of Virginia City and 15 miles east of Dillon. Ruby Point, 9,391' is the highest point. More than half of this dry country lies above 8,000'.

BLACKTAIL MOUNTAINS

This range extends 20 miles southeast of Dillon, and boasts several 8,000' peaks. A 12-mile-long plateau, dissected by deep timbered canyons with shear headwalls and cliffs, dominates much of the Blacktails. The central part of the plateau, Blacktail Mountain, contains a barely discernible high point of 9,477'.

TENDOY MOUNTAINS

The Tendoys stretch northward just beyond Lima for 30 miles and receive heavy motorized use, although an almost 70,000-acre eastern segment—extending for 20 miles along the crest of the

Each range has its own *characteristics*

and *places* to explore.

Harkness
Lake reflects
Eighteenmile and
Cottonwood Pks.
GEORGE WUERTHNER

range—is roadless. Dixon Mountain, 9,674', is the most prominent and highest landmark in the Tendoys. Sourdough Peak at 9,571' is the second-highest summit.

LIMA PEAKS

Just northwest of Monida Pass and the Montana-Idaho line, the Lima Peaks, or the Garfield Peaks as they're sometimes called, soar to more than 10,000'. Garfield Mountain, 10,961', towers above dry grassland. The landscape in these parts is about 80 percent void of trees. Glaciers have carved cirques out of the north face of the range. Little Sheep Creek separates these southwest Montana points from the main range of the Bitterroot/Beaverhead Mountains and an area called the Red Conglomerate Peaks.

THE HIGHLANDS

Butte's mountains are prominent from the mining city, especially for cars coming down the hill on I-15 from Elk Park into the city. Table Mountain, a plateau-like summit at 10,223', is their highest point.

Highland Mtns. south of Butte.
JOHN LAMBING

Upper Yaak Falls in the Purcell Mtns.
SALVATORE VASAPOLLI

Expedition Lake
in the Hilgard
Basin, Madison
Range.
RICK AND SUSIE GRAETZ

THE MADISON RANGE AND LEE METCALF WILDERNESS

Twenty miles beyond Bozeman, Montana's second-highest mountain range, the Madison, begins its climb from the Gallatin Canyon. It then heads south for almost 50 miles before abruptly dropping off at Hebgen and Quake lakes, near Yellowstone National Park. Along the way, east-flank waters are sent into the Gallatin River, and snowmelt from its western slopes feeds the Madison River.

Six peaks top 11,000', including 11,316' Hilgard, the highest in Montana outside the Beartooth. Almost 120 of the apexes are higher than 10,000', and 74 of those still are unnamed. The range comprises several groupings: the Spanish Peaks; Fan, Lone, Cedar and Sphinx mountains; the Taylor Peaks; the Hilgard area; the Monument Peaks. Rugged east-west canyons starting below the Madison divide separate them. Lush meadows and high, open, grassy basins characterize the terrain surrounding the summits.

Much of this high-country-splendor complex is in the federally protected Lee Metcalf Wilderness Area.

On the range's north end, in the Spanish Peaks, 25 points reach above 10,000', with Gallatin, at 11,105', the highest. Extensive glaciation is evident in this very rugged high country. One of Montana's greatest elevation gains is found on the northwest side: the rise from Bear Trap Canyon and Cowboy's Heaven on the Madison River, to the crest of the Spanish Peaks, at 6,500'.

The Fan and Lone Mountain area is the only place in this Madison chain where a road reaches and crosses the hydrological divide. A private byway in the Big Sky Resort area passes it through Jack Creek. This drainage also separates the Spanish Peaks segment of the Lee Metcalf from its southern extension. Just south of Lone Mountain and Big Sky, the distinct form of 10,876' Sphinx marks the skyline.

Below the Sphinx, the Taylor Peaks, with 11,256' Koch Peak, accentuate one of the least-visited regions of the Madison Range. Just to the south of 11,202' Imp Peak and the Taylor summits, the basins of the Hilgard Peaks present one of Montana's most beautiful alpine displays. Of the more than 70 lakes that grace the Madison Range, most are found in these southern reaches. This segment of the mountains, as well as the Spanish Peaks, receives heavy use, especially from horse parties. And as it is some of the area's roughest landscape, with significant altitude gains, hikers earn their way.

The Monument Peak area is set apart from the main range in the southeast corner of the uplift. In essence, it is an island of wilderness separated from the Taylor-Hilgard region by the Cabin Creek Special Management Area.

The Lee Metcalf Wilderness Area, named after one of Montana's greatest U.S. senators, includes 254,944 acres of the range. Senator Metcalf was a tireless supporter of protecting Montana's wild lands, and his passing left a void in American conservation that has not yet been filled. He represented Montana in the U.S. Congress for more than 25 years and emerged as a giant in the struggle to preserve a portion of the nation's heritage. Without him, much of our treasured wilderness would have long ago been destroyed. He was a man to match Montana's mountains.

More than 586 Montana summits

exceed 10,000'; 60 surpass 11,000';

and 27 eclipse 12,000' in height.

From Coffin Mtn.
looking to Lionhead
Mtn. and Baldy Pk.
on the Montana/
Idaho border.
SALVATORE VASAPOLLI

GALLATIN RANGE

The summits of one of Montana's great hiking areas, the Gallatin Range, rise to more than 10,000' and are bordered by the Gallatin Canyon to the west and the Yellowstone River and Paradise Valley to the east. Bozeman and the Gallatin Valley form the range's northern boundary. The massif extends into Yellowstone National Park as it heads south for 60 miles. Wildlife managers consider its peaks and meadows to be some of America's very best elk country, and essential as wintering and calving range for the large north Yellowstone elk herd. Hyalite Peak, 10,299', and Ramshorn Peak, 10,289', are two of its highest summits.

TOBACCO ROOT MOUNTAINS

Southeast of Butte, the Tobacco Roots are a tight cluster of 10,000' peaks, with numerous lakes and extensive signs of past mining activity. Twenty-eight pinnacles reach higher than 10,000'. Mount Jefferson, 10,600', is the highest summit.

GRAVELLY RANGE

The Gravellys are a rolling plateau-like range to the south of Virginia City and just west of the Madison Range and Madison River. At 10,545', Black Butte, the highest summit, is a distinctive landmark stretching above subalpine grassland.

GREENHORN RANGE

These mountains are a small subrange of the Gravellys, with a high point of 9,967', located northwest of the main range and southwest of Virginia City.

SNOWCREST RANGE

A little known but beautiful mountain complex, the Snowcrest is separated from the Gravellys to the east by the relatively narrow canyon of the Ruby River. 10,581' Sunset Peak is its highest reach. It's a mix of alpine meadows, sagebrush foothills, dense timber and wooded windswept ridges. Both the Gravellys and the Snowcrest border the Centennial Valley and Red Rock Lakes National Wildlife Refuge to the south. Several other peaks in this 25-mile-long range soar above 10,000', including 10,220' Antone Peak and 10,486' Olson Peak. Several other summits come close to, or exceed, 10,000'. Trails crisscross this range that can be reached from Dillon or Sheridan.

THE LIONHEAD MOUNTAINS

Some folks consider the Lionheads to be a southern extension of the Madison Range, separated from it by the steep canyon of the Madison River and Quake Lake. Others call these the Henry's Lake Mountains. They are just west of West Yellowstone and contain peaks over 10,000' including their highest, 10,600' Sheep Point. Most of the Lionhead is in Idaho. Nine subalpine lakes sparkle among some high cirques.

44

Castle Mtns.
near White
Sulphur Springs.
RICK AND SUSIE GRAETZ

WEST CENTRAL MOUNTAINS

Most of the mountain groups in this area aren't well known and don't receive as much notice as places like the Beartooth, the summits of Glacier National Park or the Bitterroot Range. But in the spirit of exploring Montana both via roads and in wild country, they're every bit as worthwhile to see. Many of them cover the state's early-day heritage, especially the large cluster of mountains and hills yet to be named between Helena and Deer Lodge. For a change, try wandering places such as the Sapphires, the John Longs and the Little Belts. It'll be interesting and you'll find surprises.

LITTLE BELT MOUNTAINS

Located southeast of Great Falls, the Little Belts are 70 miles across and 60 miles from north to south, reaching from the Smith River on the west to Judith Gap below their east side. They're known for logging, mining, Yogo sapphires and skiing; Showdown, Montana's oldest downhill ski area, is just above King's Hill Pass in the center of the massif.

A few of their broad peaks rise over 8,000'. Mount Baldy, 9,175', and Yogo Peak, 8,801', are the highest. Two of Montana's most fantastic wild places, the Middle Fork of the Judith River and the Tender Foot/Deep Creek area, are in these mountains.

CASTLE MOUNTAINS

The Castles rise between the Little Belts and the Crazy Mountains and are above White Sulphur Spring's southeast side. Many relics of mining days can be found here. The town of Castle, born on a silver boom, stands as a true ghost town. Igneous spires that resemble turrets of a chateau give the area its name. Several peaks are over 8,000'—including 8,566' Elk Peak, the highest point.

BIG BELT MOUNTAINS

The Missouri River and Canyon Ferry Lake lie below their steep west slopes while the east side rolls down toward the Smith River Valley. The Big Belts are 80 miles long and known for their deep limestone canyons especially the Gates of the Mountains. Its highest summits are Mount Baldy, 9,472', and Mount Edith at about 9,480'. Gates of the Mountains Wilderness Area and Beartooth Wildlife Management Area are in the northern end. On the south, Birch Creek Basin is guarded by Baldy and Edith peaks and holds about 12 lakes.

ADEL MOUNTAINS

They are a northern extension of the Big Belts above Craig and Wolf Creek on their east side. Many volcanic formations in the Adels result in flat-topped buttes. Sieben Point, 7,093', is the highest one.

ELKHORN MOUNTAINS

These are Helena's hunting grounds and a wild landscape enjoying designation as a "special wildlife management unit," owing to its large elk population. They're considered to be the most productive elk habitat in Montana. The two highest summits, Crow Peak at 9,414' and Elkhorn Peak at 9,381', are connected by a ridge. Several other peaks are over 8,000'. Although not considered a true ghost town, as a few people still live there, the town of Elkhorn is a remnant of a colorful

46

Missouri River
Gates of the
Mtns., Big Belt
Mtns.
RICK AND SUSIE GRAETZ

mining past. The McClellan and Beaver Creek area, closest to Helena, are the wildest parts of the range.

THE ANACONDA-PINTLER RANGE

Often called the Pintlers, two-thirds of this range is protected by the magnificent Anaconda Pintler Wilderness Area. A 40-mile stretch of the Continental Divide serves as its backbone. Many peaks in the wilderness are well over 10,000', culminating in 10,793' West Goat Peak, the loftiest point.

Two of the nation's finest trout streams, Rock Creek and The Big Hole River, gather some of their headwaters from these upper reaches. The lower Big Hole Valley is on its southeast flank. Anaconda and Georgetown Lake touch the chain on its northeast corner.

FLINT CREEK RANGE

With just one peak exceeding 10,000' (10,168' Mt. Powell), the Flint Creeks are the 13th-highest range in the state. The highest summits are all clustered in one roadless area near Powell. Many other tops exceed 8,000'–9,000'. Deer Lodge and the Clark Fork River Valley are on the east. with the Philipsburg area to the west. The range is 25 miles long and has many remains of early mining, including buildings of the old silver town, Granite.

Discovery Basin Ski Area is in the southwest corner, just above Georgetown Lake.

THE SAPPHIRE RANGE

Eighty-five miles long, this mass of mountains forms the entire eastern boundary of the Bitter-root Valley. Steep walls of Rock Creek Canyon are on the east side and they serve as Missoula's backdoor, with the rise of 5,158' Mt. Sentinel. In the south the Sapphires butt up against the Pintlers. Welcome Creek Wilderness Area is part of these forested mountains that support a large concentration of elk and moose. Kent Peak, at just a bit over 9,000', is their highest point. Quite a few other tops and ridgelines exceed 8,000'.

The scenic Skalkaho Road crosses the range in the south, heading east from Hamilton to the Georgetown Lake area.

JOHN LONG MOUNTAINS

Rock Creek separates the John Longs from the Sapphires on the west, and the Flint Creek Valley near Philipsburg forms their eastern perimeter. They're 30 miles long and have very few summits over 7,000'. An 8,468' point just east of Quigg Peak is the highest top. Black Pine at 7,937' and Pine Ridge at 7,932' are two other high areas.

GARNET RANGE

The Garnets have been heavily mined. The ghost towns of Garnet and Coloma stand as silent sentinels of the gold and silver era. There peaks and hills have dense timber stands.

They trend east-west for 60 miles, with the Clark Fork bordering their south edge and the Blackfoot River the north. Logging and mining have created many roads wanderering throughout the range.

Most of the peaks are between 6,000'–7,000'. On the eastern end and north of Gold Creek, they go well over 7,000' with 7,511' Mt. Baldy being the highest.

UNNAMED MOUNTAINS

There is no official name for the wide expanse of mountains that extends from Lincoln and the Blackfoot Valley, in the north, to Butte and Elk Park in the south. The Helmville and Deer Lodge valleys form their western boundary, and the valley of Prickly Pear Creek and the Boulder Valley guard the east. The Helena Valley is in its northeast corner. The Continental Divide meanders through it. Some maps have their own monikers for certain parts of it, such as the Deer Lodge Mountains on the east and the Boulder Mountains farther in.

For a lack of better name, we'll call them Montana's Heritage Mountains, as they have remnants of almost all of Montana's past—including logging, mining, early-day skiing and untouched wildlands. Highway 12 at MacDonald Pass crosses them in the center, and I-15 skirts their southern end on its way from Helena to Butte.

There are roadless areas such as Nevada Mountain, Blackfoot Meadows and the Sheep Head region. The old backroad passes of Fletcher and Stemple cross it in the northeast, and the Great Divide Ski Area slopes downward from Mt. Belmont.

Black Mountain, Nevada Mountain and Thunderbolt Peaks are all over 8,000'.

48

Skalkaho Falls
in the Sapphire
Mtns.
JOHN REDDY

Big Snowy Mtns.
near Lewistown.
RICK AND SUSIE GRAETZ

MONTANA'S MOUNTAINS EAST OF THE NORTHERN ROCKIES

Ranges in central and eastern Montana are often called "island mountains." From high points, they appear in the distance as an archipelago of islands adrift in the vast sea of the Montana prairie.

Each uplift is unique and adds to the beauty of the high plains. They contain diverse communities of wildlife and vegetation, and provide sanctuary from the midsummer heat of lower country. Their elevation allows them to garner more moisture than the surrounding prairie and, therefore, their environment comes close to that of the Rocky Mountains farther west.

THE BIG SNOWY MOUNTAINS

The Big Snowy Mountains ascend in an elongated mass from the ocean of prairie lands of central Montana…a distinct range with a perch that looks out on the farthest-reaching views in Big Sky Country. This unique mountain complex is located 15 miles south of Lewistown, the geographic center of the state. Instead of a rugged summit line, an eight-mile-long, tundra-like meadow, over 8,200' high, makes up a large portion of the top. One lengthy stretch, a narrow smooth spine, is appropriately called Knife Blade Ridge. From the Snowies highest point, 8,681' Greathouse Peak, on a day when the air is clear, a hiker can survey a 300-mile span from the Sweetgrass Hills near Shelby in the northwest, to the Beartooth and Pryor mountains below the Yellowstone River Country to the south and southeast.

Porous limestone makes up these east-west aligned mountains and allows rain and snowmelt to seep down through them into an aquifer that pours out in several springs; including Big Springs, which supplies Lewistown with its water, reportedly the purest in the nation. Deep bowl-like canyons and sparse tree cover characterize the dry south side of the Snowies. North-face canyons are longer, have a somewhat gentler rise, and are heavily forested.

In the western end of the Big Snowies, caves have been etched out of the limestone. Many smaller ones are still unexplored. The largest of the known caverns, Big Ice Cave, just below the top ridge, is a treat on hot summer days…the temperature inside is 40° cooler than outside. From a five-by-ten-foot entry, the cave slopes downward to a room about 100' long and 75' wide. Refrigeration comes from a heavily compacted icy snow drift that lasts the year around. This underground wonder is accessed from Neil Creek on the southern perimeter.

Popular Crystal Lake, on the north, is reached by Rock Creek Road, off Montana Highway 200 west of Lewistown. From here, a trail leads to another prominent cave, Devil's Chute. A footpath off this route also heads to the nearby Big Ice Cave. Sharp eyes will spot marine fossils all around the caves.

Farther east, Half Moon Creek Trail approaches the Snowies' divide from the north, and Swimming Woman Canyon Trail reaches it via the southern flank. Both byways meet near Greathouse Peak and just west of 8,678' Old Baldy, the second-highest summit. The north-side Cottonwood Creek Trail, which follows the East Fork of Cottonwood Creek to Greathouse Peak, and a ridge route from the east slopes of the range to Old Baldy, are two other worthwhile walks. Once winter's snowbanks melt, the terrain up high is dry, so backpackers planning on overnight stays along the crest need to carry their water with them.

With the exception of the Crystal Lake area and caves, the Snowies receive low use. Their outstanding wilderness characteristics have allowed a 104,000-acre core area to be set aside as a Wilderness Study Area by the U.S. Congress. Hawks, golden and bald eagles, moose, deer, elk, goats, and bear thrive in the pristine and quiet environment of these mountains' high country.

THE LITTLE ROCKIES

Indians migrating through this territory north of the Missouri River called them "the island mountains." From a distance they resemble atolls rising from the ocean of the Great Plains. Although not very lofty (the highest point is 5,720' Antoine Butte), they reach 2,500' above the surrounding prairie and can be seen from 75 miles away. To the people in towns like Roy and Malta, this 50-square-mile mass of igneous and sedimentary rock is a favored landmark.

Much of early-day Montana can be described as being the Wild West, but the Little Rocky Mountains and the country rolling south into the Missouri Breaks were perhaps the epitome of the Old West that has been etched on movie screens. A little over 100 years ago, the characters of those times... cattle barons, gold seekers, outlaws, cowboys, vigilantes, rustlers and horse thieves went about their ways here. And before they were forced off the land, the free-roaming Plains Indians hunted enormous bison herds that passed in the shadow of these mountains.

Gold brought the white man into the Little Rockies' gulches. There are records of an 1868 discovery, but mining didn't begin until the finding of "color" in Alder Gulch in 1884, where a rough-and-tumble gold camp was established. When the placer strike didn't pan out, the place quieted down to only a few tenacious prospectors.

The Little Rockies' beginning as a roaring, almost lawless, frontier outpost—fueled by the shiny nuggets of small placer claims—soon evolved into a rich mining district. This mineral extraction business culminated in 1979 with Pegasus Gold's development of a large mine. In 1998, though, bankruptcy shut it down. Today, reclamation of the mine is underway.

Most of the land in the Little Rocky Mountains is part of the Fort Belknap Indian Reservation, home to the Assiniboine and Gros Ventre tribes. The Gros Ventres live along the mountains in the Hays-Lodgepole area, while the Assiniboine have settled at Fort Belknap Agency along the Milk River to the north.

While they did use it for vision quests, earlier Indian tribes feared the island range, because they believed bad spirits lived there. Eagle Child and Mission Peak were, and still are, sacred to the Gros Ventres. Tribal medicine men climbed them to fast and meditate. Legend has it that no one ever stayed beyond three days...terrifying visions forced them to retreat.

THE SWEETGRASS HILLS

Sacred ground to the Blackfeet Nation, three high buttes—West, Gold and East—are beacons in the country north of Chester and Shelby. West and East buttes are just under 7,000', and Gold Butte—or Middle Butte as it is sometimes called—is 6,512' above sea level. Together the hills rise 3,500' above the surrounding farmlands.

Mountains are *beloved*

landmarks to the folks

who live and work within their far ranging sight.

The Sweetgrass
Hills can be seen
from more than
75 miles away.
RICK AND SUSIE GRAETZ

BEARS PAW MOUNTAINS

This 50-mile-long collection of buttes and volcano remnants dominates the prairie just to the southeast of Havre. Bears Paw Baldy at 6,916' is the highest point. Relief in the area ranges from 1,000' to 3,000'. All of the land is on private ground, although public roads bisect it. Beaver Creek State Park, a prairie oasis of water, wildlife, and vegetation on the northern end, just out of Havre, is owned by Hill County.

HIGHWOOD MOUNTAINS

Used by the Blackfeet Indians as vantage points to spot bison herds, these mountains—east of Great Falls and rising to 7,000', are believed to be remnants of ancient volcanoes. Their highest point is Highwood Baldy at 7,625'. When the Lewis and Clark Expedition first saw them in 1805, they mistakenly thought these were the Rocky Mountains.

JUDITH MOUNTAINS

Northeast of Lewistown, 6,400' Judith Peak is the tallest summit in the Judiths. A road ascends to its top and offers fantastic views of surrounding Judith Basin country. The semi-ghost town of Maiden, once a booming gold and silver community, is also reached via this route.

In the late 1800s and early 1900s, the Judiths were heavily mined. It is almost impossible to wander through them now without stumbling upon reminders of that era.

THE MOCCASIN MOUNTAINS

Separated into north and south segments by Warm Springs Creek, these high hills are just to the northwest of Lewistown and across the valley from the Judiths. With the exception of their apexes that are BLM ground, the surrounding country is in private ownership. The highest points are about 5,600'.

LITTLE SNOWY MOUNTAINS

An eastern and lower offshoot of the Big Snowy Mountains, extending 12 miles in an east west axis to the southeast of Lewistown, their highest elevation is just under 5,800'.

BULL MOUNTAINS

This 50-mile-long range of low mountains and hills is just south of Roundup and north of Billings. Its highest points are just a bit over 4,000'. The Bulls, once heavily timbered, have been ravaged by fires in recent years. Their sandstone benches separate the Missouri and the Yellowstone river basins, and provide water to the Mussellshell River. Most of this country is in private ownership, and rough public roads traverse them.

Black Butte and
the Judith Mtns.
LARRY MAYER

WOLF MOUNTAINS

On some maps, these mountains on the eastern edge of the Crow Indian Reservation, south of Hardin, are split into the Rosebuds on the north and the Wolf Mountains in the south, but most maps show them as being one 50-mile-long, low-lying chain called the Wolfs. Several summits range between 5,000' and 5,500' in elevation, but most only reach 4,000' to 5,000'.

Dense forest interspersed with huge parklands provides good grazing and wildlife habitat. The eastern side, sloping off to the Tongue River Valley, has particularly beautiful wildflower shows in the spring and summer. From points on the western fringe, it's possible to look out across much of Crow Country.

CHALK BUTTES AND EKALAKA HILLS

A mixed collection of buttes and hills, the Chalk Buttes ascend to just over 4,000' in elevation and 700' above the prairie floor. The adjacent and lower Ekalaka Hills rise gradually to steep overlooks of the prairie to the south.

THE LONG PINES

Just south and east of the Ekalaka Hills, the Long Pines rise to 700' above surrounding landscape, and to elevations close to 4,500'. At one time, this extreme eastern portion of the Custer National Forest had a heavy cover of ponderosa pine. Recent fires, though, have taken out many of the trees and opened up the country. Capital Rock, on the Long Pines' eastern side, is a mass of white volcanic ash resembling the nation's capitol. It is protected as a monument by the U.S. Forest Service, and primitive roads reach it.

BLUE MOUNTAIN

This high point just off of the North Dakota line between Sidney and Glendive is 800' higher than the remote prairie it overlooks. At a whopping 3,084' in elevation, it is the tallest point in northeastern Montana.

SHEEP MOUNTAINS

The Little and Big Sheep mountains are a series of hills and eroded badlands between Circle and Glendive. Their highest point at 3,625', is no more than 300' above the adjacent country.

Rimrocks in the
Ekalaka Hills.
SALVATORE VASAPOLLI

Jackson Glacier,
GNP.
RICK AND SUSIE GRAETZ

MONTANA'S MOUNTAIN GLACIERS

Well back in time, perhaps about 10,000 years ago, what is today's Big Sky Country experienced a much colder and snowier climate than we now enjoy. During various ice ages, many of our mountain ranges were almost entirely engulfed in snow and ice. The Flathead Valley near Kalispell, as an example, was filled with ice, perhaps as much as 3,000' deep. Ice spilled from Glacier Park past Browning, and met a continental glacier flowing south from Canada. The Canadian intrusion extended to the present location of the Missouri River in the eastern half of our state.

Miniature remnants of that period still cling to walls and occupy cirques (steep walled, half-bowl–shaped basins) in some of our higher mountains. An estimated 37 active alpine glaciers are in Glacier National Park, several in the Mission Mountains, one in the Cabinets, two in the Flathead Range, one in the Swan Range, one in the Crazies and many (not yet counted) in the Absaroka-Beartooth Mountains.

Most of these ice age relics are visible only to the backcountry visitor. In Glacier, though, some can be glimpsed from the road. Jackson and Blackfoot glaciers can be seen from above St. Mary Lake on the Going-To-The-Sun Road, Old Sun on Mt. Merritt is visible from near Babb, and a pullout at the Apikuni Creek Trailhead brings into view Salamander and Gem glaciers in the Many Glacier region.

Several of these icy features are relatively well known. Jackson and Blackfoot glaciers in Glacier are so because of their roadway viewpoints and sizes. Blackfoot, at 430 acres, is the Park's largest. Grinnell Glacier (217 acres) near the Many Glacier region, and Sperry Glacier (220 acres) are visited by hundreds of trekkers every year via easy trails. Grasshopper Glacier in the Absaroka-Beartooth Wilderness Area, on the north side of the ridge between Iceberg Peak, and Mt. Wilse, at the head of the West Rosebud Drainage, are destinations for many hikers. The place takes its name from the millions of grasshoppers embedded in the glacial ice. It is believed that these migratory insects were passing over the Beartooth more than 200 years ago, when a storm caught them and deposited them on the building glacier.

Late summer is the best time to see actual glaciers. Most of their masses are free of new snow. Blue ice sliced by crevasses and strewn with mud and rock stands out.

Perennial snowfields in the high country are often mistaken for glaciers. A true glacier moves and needs to be at least 65' deep and 25 acres in size. The process—more deposition of snow in the cold season than melting in summer, coupled with continued melting and freezing—turns the body into ice. As it thickens, more weight is added to the lower ice layers. And when the glacier forms on steep slopes, as is the case in Montana, gravity causes the underlying strata to move. Late spring and early summer are when the maximum new snow load is reached, and the most movement occurs. Each ice body has its own characteristic but, on the average in the Northern Rockies, flow is probably no more than an inch or two a day. In coastal Alaska, a glacier could form in ten years but in the drier Northern Rockies it would take much longer

Rock glaciers are found in more places than are the solid snow and ice variety. Aside from in the ranges mentioned above, rock glaciers are also active in the Madison, Pioneer, Bitterroot and Pintler ranges. Rocks cover and insulate buried ice. Only colder dense air is absorbed within the conglom-

Terminus of
the Glacier
Pk. Glacier
and Lake of
the Clouds,
Mission
Mtns.
RICK AND SUSIE
GRAETZ

In the
Whitefish
Range looking
into Glacier
National Park.
RICK AND SUSIE GRAETZ

eration helping to keep the ice intact. Rock glaciers flow very slowly and have steep fronts with rippled surfaces.

Glaciers of the past have, especially in Montana's alpine regions, left behind a legacy of good work. They sculptured our mountains into the beautiful forms we see today. Their movement and former presence left behind lake-filled cirques, deep U-shaped canyons, and hanging valleys from which waterfalls plunge. Their abrasive surface action can be seen in long striations carved into bedrock. And rock flour, a product of their grinding activity, gives a milky color to glacial lake surfaces that turn aqua when sunlight filters through.

All of Montana's glaciers are shrinking. Projections are that, given current weather trends, by the year 2030 they will be completely gone from Glacier National Park.

Will the glaciers come back again? Only a trend towards an overall colder and wetter climate would ensure their return. Some folks feel it would be a good thing if they come back; urban sprawl would be halted and the ski season would be more predictable and last longer.

Flathead Range
in the Great Bear
Wilderness,
Hungry Horse
Reservoir.
CHUCK HANEY

Arrowleaf
balasmroot colors
mountainsides
and fields.
JOHN REDDY

Grotto Falls,
Hyalite Creek—
Gallatin Range.
JOHN REDDY

67

Ear Mtn.
on the Rocky
Mountain Front.
RICK AND SUSIE GRAETZ

Rainbow Lake
in the Salish Mtns.
RICK AND SUSIE GRAETZ

Sawtooth Ridge
on the Rocky
Mountain Front.
JOHN LAMBING

The appearance of the island mountains on the horizon

is a signal to locals that home is near.

Sheep Creek in the
Little Belt Mtns.
RICK AND SUSIE GRAETZ

Big Hole Valley
and the Beaverhead
Mtns. in the
Bitterroot Range.
RICK AND SUSIE GRAETZ

Crazy Mtns.
RICK AND SUSIE GRAETZ

A familiar Glacier
National Park
scene.
RICK AND SUSIE GRAETZ

Mt. Cowan
in the Absarokas.
RICK AND SUSIE GRAETZ

Atop the Big
Snowies looking
towards Lewistown,
the Moccasins (left)
and the Judiths
(right).
RICK AND SUSIE GRAETZ

From Tower Pk.
looking at Torrey
Pk., East Pioneer
Mtns.
GEORGE WUERTHNER

Nevada Creek
and Peak area
above the
Helmville Valley.
JOHN LAMBING

Yellow tamaracks
along the Swan
Range.
RICK AND SUSIE GRAETZ

Not only beautiful, they provide us

with liquid gold...water.

Giant cedars, Ross
Creek Scenic Area
in the west
Cabinets/
Scotchman Pks.
CHUCK HANEY

Little Blackfoot
River, Flint Creek
Range.
JOHN REDDY

In the Bears
Paw Mtns.
RICK AND SUSIE GRAETZ

The Sliter farm
and the Swan Range
near Big Fork.
JOHN REDDY

Rocky
Mountain Front.
DOUGLASS DYE

Mt. Reynolds
on east side of
Logan Pass, GNP.
RICK AND SUSIE GRAETZ

The Continental Divide *twists*

and turns throughout western Montana.

Goat Flat,
Anaconda-Pintler
Wilderness.
WAYNE MUMFORD

Southern
Madison Range.
RICK AND SUSIE GRAETZ

Georgetown Lake and the edge of the Flint Creek Range looking towards the Anaconda-Pintlers.
JOHN REDDY

Little Rockies
from the historic
Matador Ranch.
RICK AND SUSIE GRAETZ

Tobacco Root
Mtns. from the
Jefferson River
Valley.
RICK AND SUSIE GRAETZ

There are several lifetimes

worth of Montana's mountains to climb.

Below Elkhorn Pk.
in the Elkhorn
Mtns.
GEORGE WUERTHNER

Long Pines south-
east of Ekalaka.
RICK AND SUSIE GRAETZ

Gallatin River
and the Gallatin
Range.
RICK AND SUSIE GRAETZ

Lone Mtn. in the
Madison Range,
Big Sky area.
RICK AND SUSIE GRAETZ

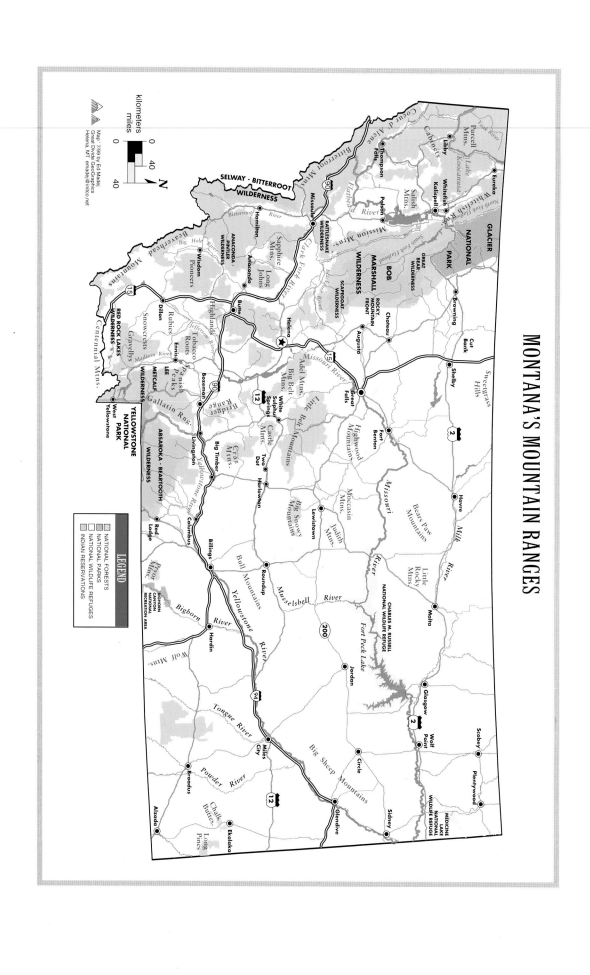

MONTANA'S MOUNTAIN RANGES

LEGEND
- NATIONAL FORESTS
- NATIONAL PARKS
- NATIONAL WILDLIFE REFUGES
- INDIAN RESERVATIONS

kilometers
miles

0   40

0   40

N

Map 7/99 by Ed Madej
Great Divide GeoGraphics
Helena, MT emadej@in|co.net